£7.99
A
GN

ART ATTACK

even more COOL STUFF!

DK

LONDON, NEW YORK, MELBOURNE,
MUNICH and DELHI

Project Editors Selina Wood, Penelope York, Julia March
Senior Art Editors Carole Oliver, Anne Sharples
Designer Jacqueline Gooden

Model Makers Jim Copley, Anne Sharples
Photography Steve Gorton, Gary Ombler,
Stephen Oliver, Andy Crawford
Illustration Dorian Spencer Davies

Managing Editor Mary Ling
Managing Art Editor Rachael Foster
Production Orla Creegan, Vivianne Cracknell
DTP Designers Almudena Díaz, Lauren Egan
Jacket Designer Anne Sharples

Published in Great Britain in 2005 by
Dorling Kindersley Limited
80 Strand, London WC2R 0RL
5 6 7 8 10 9 7 5 3 1

Copyright © 2005 Dorling Kindersley Limited
Art Attack © The Media Merchants TV Company Limited 2005
A HIT Entertainment Company. All Rights Reserved

Material in this edition has appeared previously in the following books:
Art Attack Annual 2001 © 2000 Dorling Kindersley Limited
Art Attack Secret Stuff © 2000 Dorling Kindersley Limited

A CIP catalogue record for this book
is available from the British Library.

ISBN: 0-4053-1176-2

Colour reproduction by Media Development and Printing Ltd, UK
Printed and bound in China by L. Rex

Dorling Kindersley would like to thank everyone at
Media Merchants for their help and enthusiasm.
www.artattack.co.uk

discover more at
www.dk.com

CONTENTS

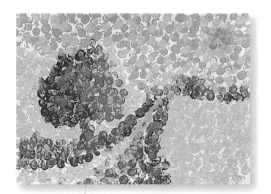

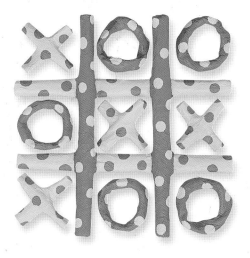

INTRODUCTION

Welcome to Art Attack: Even More Cool Stuff! This book is jam-packed with the best Art Attacks ever. There are invisible maps, crackproof codes, plaques for your bedroom door, number plates for your bike and lots more brilliant projects. You'll be modelling, printing, lettering and using eye-popping paint effects. You should find it easy to get your hands on all of the materials used in this book, so you can get started right away. Best of all, anyone can make these Art Attacks so don't worry if you think you're no good at art. What are you waiting for? Grab your paints and pencil, have fun – and have an Art Attack!

Crayons

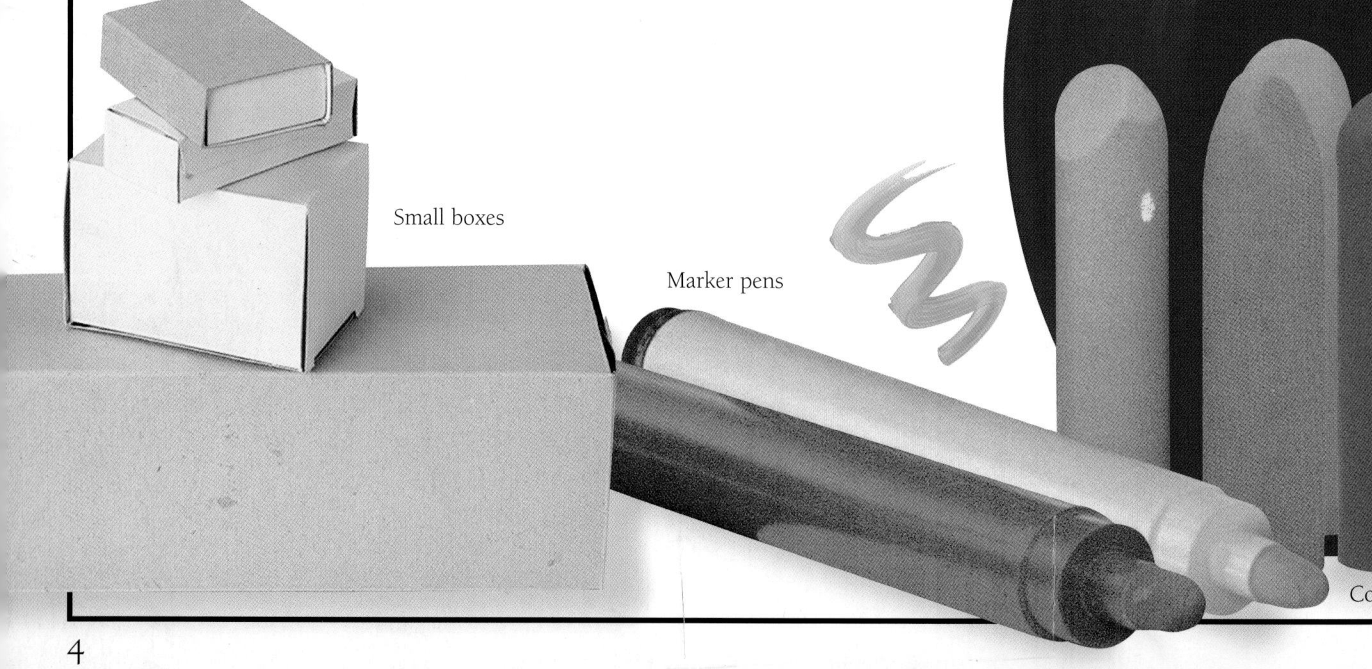

PVA glue

Small boxes

Marker pens

Coloured chalks

Acrylic paint

Paint

You will need three different kinds of paint for the projects in this book: acrylic, poster, and watercolour. Use a palette or old plate to mix your colours.

Paint palette

Hints and tips

• Make sure you open the windows when you use marker pens.
• Thick cardboard is easier to cut if you wet it slightly with water.
• Emphasize details on your models by outlining them in thick, black marker pen.
• A balloon pump is a quick and easy way to blow up balloons.
• When you sprinkle glitter over a project, lay a piece of paper underneath so that you can pour excess glitter back into the pot.

Split pins

Sticky tack

Sticky tape

Protractor

Lolly stick

Pencil

Fine marker pen

Paintbrush

Ruler

Scissors

Kitchen towel and toilet paper

Sticky-backed plastic

Kitchen foil

Glitter

Cardboard

Use different size plates as templates for perfect circles.

White card

Coloured paper

Newspaper

Poster paint

PAPIER POWER

Papier-mâché is a brilliant material for moulding 3-D models. Here are some helpful tips and ideas for generating papier-mâché power!

You will need

1 part water (e.g. one tablespoon)

2 parts PVA glue (e.g. two tablespoons – twice as much as the water)

Strips of kitchen towel or newspaper

How to make papier-mâché

Prepare your glue mixture by adding one part water to every two parts PVA glue. Tear up some strips of loo roll, kitchen towel, or newspaper. Cover your model with glue mixture, and lay the strips on top. As you build up layers, keep adding more glue mixture on top with a paintbrush. You will need at least three layers on the model and don't worry about it getting messy – when it has dried overnight it will be stiff and rock hard!

Balloon base

Balloons are a great base for making head-shaped models. Just add four layers of newspaper papier-mâché and when the mould is dry, you can pop the balloon. You are then left with an oval mould. If you want to add facial features to a papier-mâché mask, mould them from a pulp mixture of tissue and PVA glue.

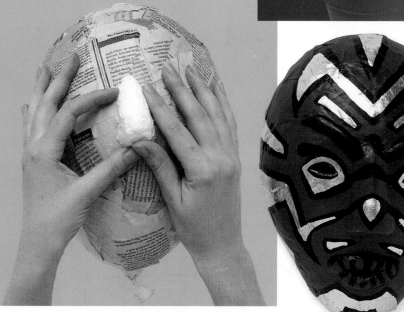

Funny face bowl

Make your own colourful bowl by adding papier-mâché to the inside of a breakfast or soup bowl.

To make it easy to separate the mould from the bowl, first cover the inside of the bowl with cling wrap. When the mould is dry, pull the bowl away from the cling wrap.

Cardboard-based snake hook

By using a base of cardboard and newpaper you can create practically any shape you like. This snake hook is made from a cardboard S shape padded out with scrunched up newspaper. Create eyes by rolling up two small newspaper balls. Then add four layers of papier-mâché mixture to mould it into shape.

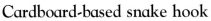

Newspaper bracelets

Make a jazzy bracelet by adding papier-mâché mixture to a ring of twisted-up newspaper. When it is dry, paint your bracelet with bright or metallic colours.

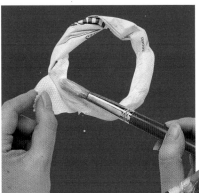

Building up your papier-mâché

Why not use a combination of different bases to make a mega model like this dinosaur money bank? This uses a balloon base for the body, cardboard for the legs, and newspaper for the neck and tail. Keep experimenting to perfect your papier-mâché!

NUMBER PLATE

Ever noticed how number plates sometimes spell out words? Try making your own plates that you can fasten onto your bike.

From card to plate

1 Take a large piece of yellow card. With a ruler and pencil draw a 30-cm x 10-cm rectangle. In capital letters, write your name or message inside the rectangle.

Draw two screw holes at each end of the number plate to make it look real.

Hold the sticky-backed plastic down as you spread it across the card slowly.

Materials

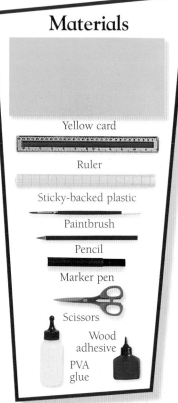

Yellow card

Ruler

Sticky-backed plastic

Paintbrush

Pencil

Marker pen

Scissors

Wood adhesive

PVA glue

2 To make the plate waterproof, carefully cover the card with sticky-backed plastic, making sure that you spread it on smoothly. Take care to get rid of any air bubbles.

Make your letters big so that they can be seen from a distance.

The marker pen dries with a shiny finish.

3 Ask an adult to help you squeeze a layer of wood adhesive over the pencil lines. Leave it to dry overnight.

4 Take a permanent marker pen and colour over all the hardened adhesive areas in black. This will create the effect of raised lettering that you find on real number plates.

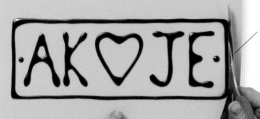

Cut the number plate out carefully with scissors.

Brush over the back of the plate with PVA glue.

5 Now you are ready to cut the number plate out. With a pair of scissors, cut around the black border, making sure you don't cut into the adhesive layer.

6 Using a brush, cover the back of the plate with a thick layer of PVA glue. This makes the back of the plate stiffer. Let the glue dry.

Colour crazy!

Why not write your name or make up some cryptic messages to go on your number plate? Then you can carefully tie it to the handlebars of your bicycle.

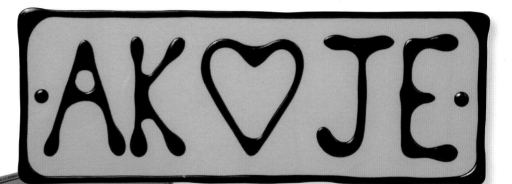

Gold and silver pens create a brilliant, glitzy effect!

How about this?
An alternative way to make your plate is by writing the glue letters straight on to the card. Then add a layer of PVA glue or varnish at the end to make it waterproof.

9

FANCY FOOTWORK

How would you like your favourite football players springing to life from your ceiling? Try these fantastic springy-limbed mobiles!

From strips to springs

Make sure the strips are exactly the same size.

Fold the bottom strip up over the top strip.

Materials

White card and coloured paper

Paint

String

Sticky tape

Scissors

Pencil

Marker pen

1 Take two pieces of different coloured paper and cut a thin, long strip from each one. Place one strip across the other to form an 'L' shape and tape them together with sticky tape.

2 Fold the paper strips over each other, until you get to the end. Fix the ends together with sticky tape. Repeat steps one and two until you have four springy strips.

Hands are very difficult to draw. If you have trouble, try drawing them with the fists clenched.

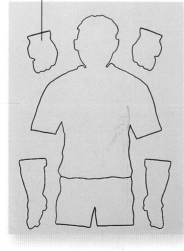

Use the colours of your favourite football team on the T-shirt.

3 Take a piece of white card and draw a body, two hands, and two legs below the knee. The bottom of the sleeves and shorts, the wrists, and the top of the socks should be the same width as the paper springs.

4 Cut out the pieces and decorate them using marker pens or paints. Colour both sides so that when you hang them up it doesn't matter which way they face. Leave them to dry overnight.

You may need quite a few pieces of sticky tape to attach them firmly.

5 Attach the hands and legs to each springy limb with sticky tape. If you want the limbs to be longer, you could always make some extra lengths with more strips and then attach them together.

Attach a piece of string to the back of the head with some tape.

Try making some 3-D hair out of some coloured paper.

6 When your springy limbs are ready, it's time to put your footballer together! Use sticky tape to attach the limbs to the arms and the shorts. Ensure that they are fixed securely.

Main man
Every footballer needs a ball to keep them occupied! Draw the shape of a ball on white card, cut it out, and attach it to a foot with sticky tape.

Team players
Why not create an entire team with their own names and numbers on their shirts? Hang them in your room and watch them spring!

ALL CHANGE

Here's a clever way to create a picture that changes from day to night in a flash. It's easy to make, and will amaze your friends!

From card to picture

Draw around a plate with a pencil.

Mark the centre point of each circle with a pencil.

Materials

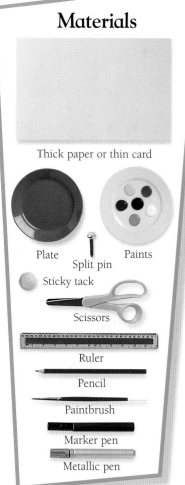

Thick paper or thin card

Plate   Paints
Split pin
Sticky tack
Scissors
Ruler
Pencil
Paintbrush
Marker pen
Metallic pen

1 Take a piece of thick paper or thin card, and a plate. Turn the plate upside-down and draw around it to make two circles. Cut them out.

2 Using a ruler and pencil, measure across each circle to find the centre. With a pencil, pierce a hole through the centre point.

Placing some sticky tack underneath, pierce a hole in the centre of each circle.

Colour in your picture with paints or marker pens.

Draw lines across the area you'll want to cut out.

3 Take one of the circles and draw a wavy horizontal line just above the centre point. This will be the horizon line for your landscape scene.

4 Draw some features, such as a house, on the horizon line. Add a landscape scene underneath. Then cut out the sky above the horizon line.

  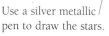 

Use a silver metallic pen to draw the stars.

Open out the split pin at the back.

5 Draw a line through the centre of your second circle. In the top half, draw a sun and some clouds, and in the bottom section, stars and a moon. Colour it with paints and metallic pens.

6 Place your landscape picture over your sky picture and push a split pin through the centre hole of both circles. Open out the split pin at the back. Now you just twirl around your picture to change day into night.

Twirl pictures

All change! See how different the landscapes look when you change the sky around. Use lots of bright, bold colours to make other fantastic pictures such as cityscapes or jungle scenes.

Use a black marker pen to add detail.

Paint large images in the foreground so that the picture jumps out at you!

Sunshine and showers

Try creating pictures where you can change the weather. Experiment with rainbows, lightning, typhoons – anything you feel like!

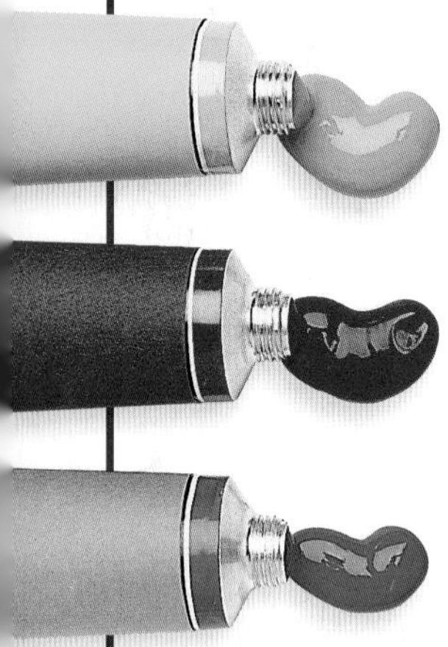

PAINT EFFECTS

Have you noticed all the different types of paints you can buy? There are brilliant things you can do with them, and that doesn't just mean painting pictures!

Multi-colours look great in wax scraping pictures.

Wax scraping with paint

You can create very striking pictures using paint and wax crayon. Cover a piece of paper with lots of colours in crayon. Next, mix some black poster paint with an equal amount of washing-up liquid. Brush the mixture over the page and leave it to dry. Then scrape out your picture with a cocktail stick. You could also use an old biro or pencil.

Try pouring two colours into the eggshell. You can create even better "plop" effects!

The best thing about wax scraping is that you never know what colour will appear next!

"Plops" away!

This paint technique is great fun! Make a 2-cm hole in an egg using a spoon handle, as if you were opening a boiled egg. Empty the contents and pour poster paint into the hole. Then, go into the garden and lay out some paper. Hold the egg high over the paper and. . . "plop" away!

Splatter effect

Start by making a stencil. Draw the shape of an animal on some coloured paper and cut it out leaving the outside in one piece. Place the stencil over some white paper. Then dip a toothbrush into some watered-down poster paint. Pull the bristles back and splatter the paint so that tiny drops land on the white paper.

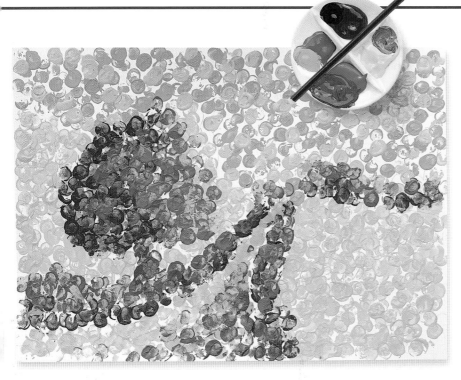

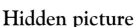

Hidden picture

Did you know you can perform magic with wax crayon and paint? First, draw a picture or message on to white paper using a white wax crayon. Wash over the drawing with watercolour paint or watered-down poster paint. Then watch your picture gradually appear!

Stipple effect

You can use the blunt end of a pencil to create this wonderful stipple effect. Dip the end of the pencil into some thick paint. Press it down on some paper to create a thick spot. Then make lots more spots that overlap so that they make shapes and features. You can create fantastic landscape scenes using this technique.

Splatter with several colours of paint to create a brilliant mottled effect.

You can paint on brightly coloured stars, stripes, and spots.

Paint your pumps

Acrylic paint will go on almost anything, even your pumps! Brighten them up by creating patterns with thick dollops of paint. They stay on the fabric even when your foot bends.

LOLLY LETTERING

H ere's a cheap and easy way to really improve your handwriting. All you need is a lolly stick and some ink to become a calligraphy wizard.

From letters to calligraphy

Watch out for any sharp bits when you snap your lolly stick.

Materials

Paper

Ruler

Pencil

Inks

Lolly sticks

Scissors

Marker pen

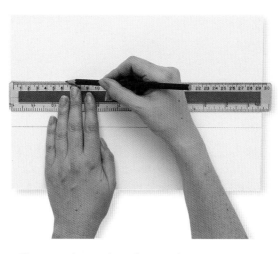

1 With a ruler, draw a line across a piece of paper. Pencil in another line along the bottom of the ruler. Move the ruler 1.5–2 cm up and draw a third line.

2 Save the stick from your favourite ice lolly and very carefully snap the stick in half. You may need to get an adult to help you.

Just dip the very end of the lolly stick into the ink.

Keep your lolly stick straight as if you were using a fountain pen.

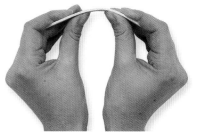

a b c d

3 Dip the broken end of one of the lolly sticks into some fountain pen ink or some poster paint mixed with lots of water.

4 Keeping the square end of the lolly stick flat on the paper, practise writing with the lolly stick. Try out different effects by altering the length and width of the strokes.

5 Sometimes when you snap a lolly stick you get a jagged edge. Don't throw this away – it can give a good split letter effect. Alternatively, you can create your own jagged edge by snipping bits of the lolly stick away with scissors.

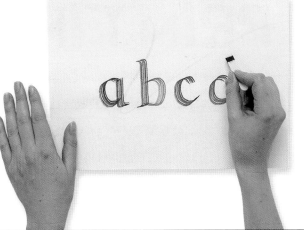

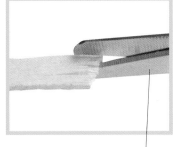

Use a pair of scissors to split the end of your lolly stick.

Calligraphy set

If you snap a lot of sticks you can make a whole set of calligraphy pens that create different styles of lettering. By snipping a notch out of the middle of the end of your stick you can create this fantastic double-lined effect.

Why not make a label to go on your bedroom door?

Posh letters

You can make some wonderful notices with your calligraphy set. Frame your notice by placing it on to coloured card and then drawing a frame around it with a marker pen.

Try writing capital letters with your lolly stick.

Press down firmly to get a clear print.

PRINTING FUN

An easy and effective way to paint lots of shapes that are all the same is by printing. It's a great way to decorate greeting cards and wrapping paper and it's also brilliant fun!

Spectacular spuds

Did you know that you can use potatoes for something a bit more artistic than eating? To make potato prints, first get an adult to help you to cut out a shape from half a large potato using a knife. Then dip the potato shape into some paint and print it on to coloured paper.

" Spuds and sponges, feet and string . . . try printing with anything you like! **"**

Use bright, bold colour paint on your string.

HAPPY

BIRTHDAY

Add your message in silver pen.

String a daisy

In pencil, draw a simple picture on thick card then cut out pieces of string and glue them on the lines of your drawing. Press the string into a plate of paint and then place it on coloured paper. Try making cool designs for birthday cards with your string prints.

18

Cardboard cut-out

Draw a bold picture, such as this dinosaur scene, on cardboard. Cut out along some of the lines, but leave some outlines in card so that you can still see what the picture is. Stick your cut-out on to another piece of cardboard and add some more details, such as eyes. Cover the image in paint, and print away!

Try and make the silver paint as even as possible.

Make sure you cover your cut-out in a thick layer of paint.

Twinkle little star

For a really glitzy effect, cut out some stars from a sponge and dip them into a plate of silver paint. Print them on to dark-coloured paper to see your stars twinkle! You can make some fantastic, festive wrapping paper using this technique.

Why not make a print of your foot on to a long envelope?

When the paint is dry you can write over the prints.

Footprint fun

Make your own personal stationery set by dipping your feet or hands into some paint and printing them on to some coloured paper and envelopes. This is messy, so it is a good idea to use washable paint, such as poster paint, and to put some plastic sheeting down first.

KRISS KROSS

D o you know someone who loves playing noughts and crosses? Why not present them with their own colourful giant-sized set?

From nought to crosses

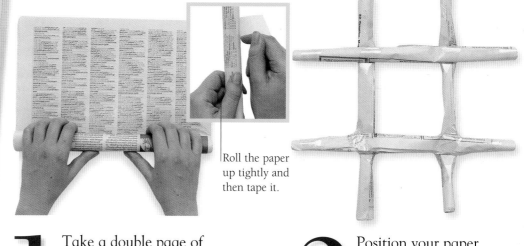

Roll the paper up tightly and then tape it.

Materials

Newspaper

Kitchen towel

Sticky tape

Paint

PVA glue

Scissors

Paintbrush

1 Take a double page of newspaper and fold it in half. Roll it into a tube and then tape it in place. Make three more of these paper tubes.

2 Position your paper tubes to form a playing grid. Then fasten the tubes together using sticky tape.

Tape the two paper pieces together to form a cross. Do this five times to make five crosses.

Twist the rolled paper between your hands.

3 Next, take another folded sheet of paper and twist it tightly from bottom to top. Make ten of these.

4 Take one of the twisted pieces of newspaper and hold it diagonally across the centre square of the playing grid. Cut off a piece to fit in the square. Do this twice and tape the two pieces together.

Once you have found the correct circle size, trim off the excess length of paper.

Dip the strips of kitchen towel into a bowl of PVA glue mixed with water (see page 14) before you lay them on the grid.

Lay the circle over the grid so that it fits into the square easily.

Cover the grid in a layer of glue mixture.

5 Curl another length of twisted paper into a circle. Position it over the playing grid to measure the correct size of the circle. Tape it together and trim off the excess. Do this five times to form five circles.

6 With a brush, spread some glue mixture over the grid. Add some strips of kitchen towel. Cover the whole grid with the strips and then add a second layer of glue mixture and kitchen towel.

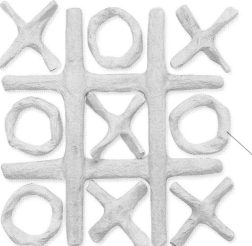

Make sure the noughts and crosses do not touch the grid or they might stick.

7 Next cover the noughts and crosses in layers of glue mixture and kitchen towel. Place them in the grid and leave the model to dry overnight.

8 Then colour all the noughts and crosses and the grid in two different colours using acrylic or poster paints. Leave them to dry.

KRISS KROSS

I f you want a noughts and crosses set that is special, why not make it multi-coloured or even replace your crosses with clay creatures?

Be careful to make pieces that fit into the grid.

Paint tip
Make sure you leave the first colour to dry before you paint on the spots.

Paint your pieces in bold, contrasting colours.

Polka dots
The good thing about these noughts and crosses is that you can paint them in your favourite colours. Or you can make them exciting by adding polka dots or stripes.

You could paint your pieces with stripes instead of these spots.

Make sure you leave your clay pieces to harden before you paint them.

Pandas and zebras

If you want an alternative to noughts and crosses, you can make pandas and zebras or any animals you like out of modelling clay. Then all you do is give them a coat of paint!

Paint the grid in spots or stripes to complement your animal faces.

You can give all your animal faces different expressions.

Use a thin brush to paint on the facial features and stripes.

BUG FOIL PLAQUE

Kitchen foil is a great art material, and you don't need a lot to create a dramatic Art Attack. Try designing one of these foil plaques!

From foil to plaque

Materials

Cardboard

Kitchen foil

PVA glue   Paint   Glue stick

Sticky tape   Toilet paper

Scissors

Ruler

Paintbrush

Marker pen

Draw thick lines to make them easy to see when you are cutting out.

Plaque border

1 Cut out two pieces of cardboard, roughly 20 cm by 15 cm. Take one of the pieces and draw a 1 cm border around the edge.

2 Use a marker pen or pencil to draw your insect inside the border, making sure it fills the whole area. Then cut out the border in one piece.

Draw an outline for each section as a cutting out guide.

Snout beetle

3 Divide your picture into small sections, as shown here. Cut out each section carefully, and glue it in position in the centre on the second piece of cardboard.

4 Next, cover one side of your border with some glue and stick it to the front of your plaque. Make sure that the border matches up with the edge of the plaque and fits neatly round the edge of your picture.

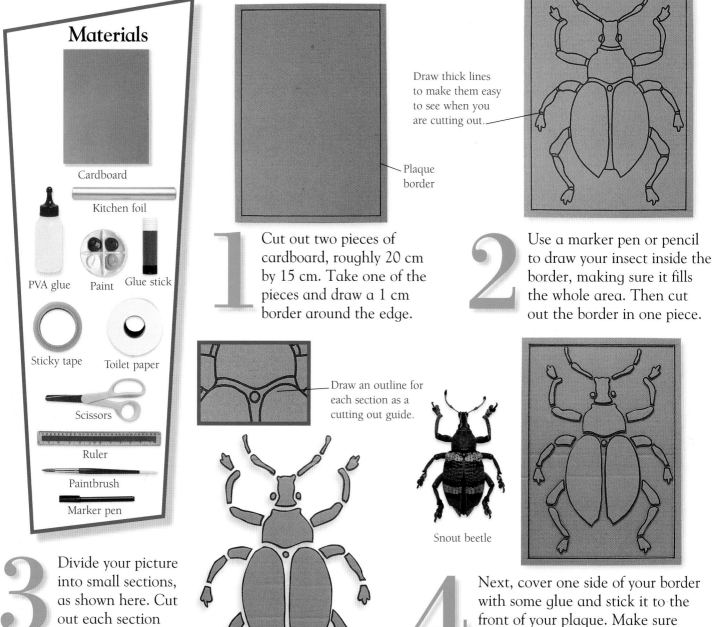

5 Brush your plaque with PVA glue and cover it with kitchen foil. Press down into the nooks and crannies with some toilet paper. Fold the edges of the foil over the back of the plaque and tape it down.

6 Water down some poster paint and brush it over the whole picture. Then take a piece of toilet paper and carefully wipe off the wet paint from the raised parts of the picture.

Creepy crawly beetle
And here it is, your very own kitchen-foil plaque. Add some extra detail to brighten up the picture, by lightly applying different colours to the silver areas when the plaque is dry. Have a go!

Number tip
If you number the sections of your bug picture before you cut them out it will help you reposition them later.

DESK SET

Do you have a desk that always seems to be untidy? Why not create a family of froggies to help keep your desk in order?

From clay to frog

1 Take two lumps of clay, one large, one small. Roll the larger piece into a ball and flatten the bottom so that it is stable. Press a paintbrush into the clay to make a deep groove.

This will be the frog's mouth.

Flatten the smaller ball of clay with the palm of your hand.

2 Roll the smaller clay piece into a ball. Squash it with your palm. With a ruler cut the clay in half vertically. Make a horizontal cut about ⅔ of the way up.

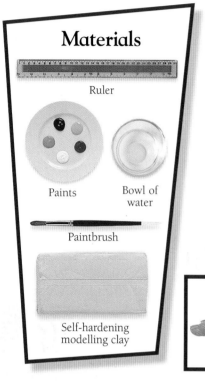

Clay tip
If your clay begins to dry out, sprinkle some water on to it so that you can mould it more easily.

Make small indentations with the end of your brush.

3 To create a webbed feet effect, use the end of a brush to mark small indentations around the edge of the clay. You now have the front and back feet.

4 Hold the ball of clay in the palm of your hand. Turn it over so that it shows the flat side, with the mouth side furthest from you. Brush some water on to the flat surface.

Materials

Ruler

Paints

Bowl of water

Paintbrush

Self-hardening modelling clay

Use a dab of water to stick the feet to the body.

Make a loop with each length of rolled clay by squeezing the ends together.

5 Take the two big feet and lay them on the back of the frog, so they stick out each side. Then, lay the two small feet underneath the mouth area. Carefully, turn the frog back over and leave it to dry.

6 Take another piece of clay and roll it into a sausage a bit longer than a finger. Do this twice to make two long, thin sausage-shaped clay strips. Bend them over to make two loops.

7 To form the frog's back legs, wet the pinched ends of the clay loops and place them in the space between the back feet and the body. Use a paintbrush to help you press them into place. Then, roll two more balls of clay to form the frog's eyes.

Make sure you attach the legs firmly before they dry.

Dab some water on to the clay balls to attach the eyes to the body.

Cover the whole of your clay model in a froggy, green colour.

8 Leave the whole frog to dry overnight so that it is rock solid. Next, paint the frog's body with green acrylic or poster paint. When the green paint is dry, paint the mouth red and the eyes white with blue irises and black pupils.

DESK SET

Your frogs are now ready for a makeover! Experiment with lots of colours, and if you like, adapt your frog into a fish or any other creature you like.

The blue irises and black pupils bring your frog to life.

Paint the inside of the mouth a bright red.

Green alert
When you have coloured the frog's body green, you can add some yellow spots to give the frog more character. Once your frog is painted, place a paintbrush or pen into the frog's mouth. It's a handy place to keep your desk items.

Make the frog's eyes shine by adding triangular highlights.

You can place long or short rulers into the frog's mouth.

MADE IN ENGLAND

Family of frogs
Make a family of frogs in different colours so that your desk top looks really colourful.

Fishy business
Why not make a fishy desk tidy? Instead of making legs and feet, mould the clay into some fins and a large tail.

Using a black marker pen, outline the spots and mouth so that they stand out.

Don't forget to add scales for a fishy effect.

Paint the fish in bright colours such as red, yellow, purple, and pink.

Big mouth
Alter the size of the mouth on each frog so that you have a desk tidy for each of your various desk items such as rulers, pencils, pens, and brushes.

Create a multi-coloured frog by adding yellow spots to its green coat.

Blues, greens, and reds look great together.

The more spots you paint, the more fun your frog will look.

BOX OF TRICKS

Do you ever have trouble knowing what to send someone special? Here's an idea, a matchbox brooch, and what's inside? . . . shhh, it's a secret!

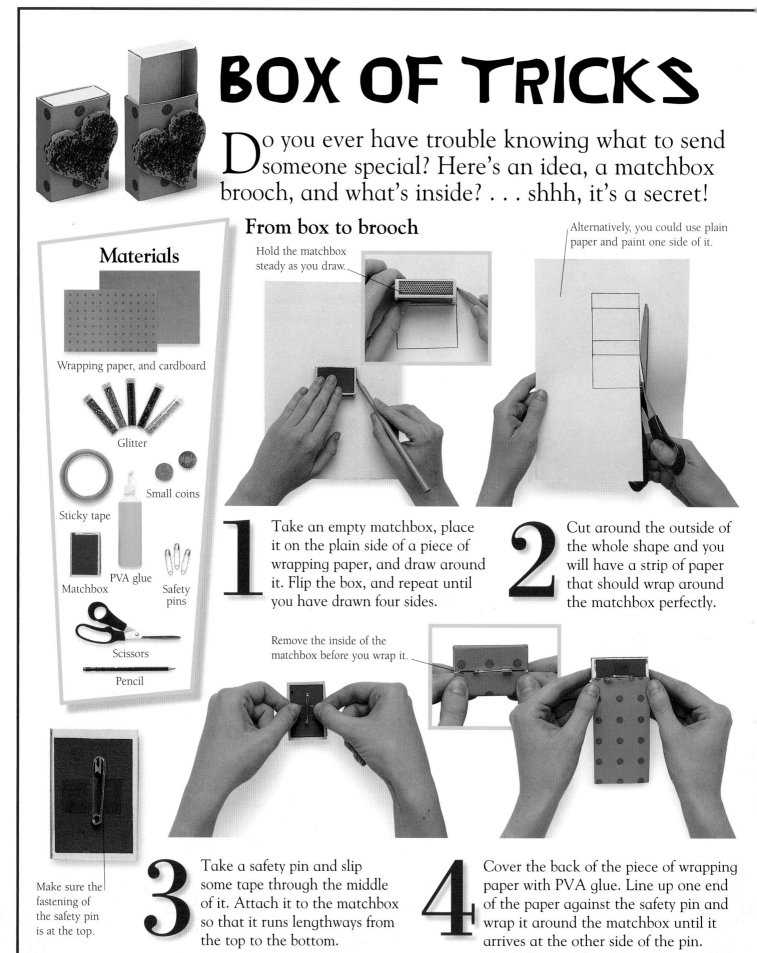

From box to brooch

Materials

Wrapping paper, and cardboard

Glitter

Small coins

Sticky tape

PVA glue

Matchbox

Safety pins

Scissors

Pencil

Hold the matchbox steady as you draw.

Alternatively, you could use plain paper and paint one side of it.

1 Take an empty matchbox, place it on the plain side of a piece of wrapping paper, and draw around it. Flip the box, and repeat until you have drawn four sides.

2 Cut around the outside of the whole shape and you will have a strip of paper that should wrap around the matchbox perfectly.

Remove the inside of the matchbox before you wrap it.

Make sure the fastening of the safety pin is at the top.

3 Take a safety pin and slip some tape through the middle of it. Attach it to the matchbox so that it runs lengthways from the top to the bottom.

4 Cover the back of the piece of wrapping paper with PVA glue. Line up one end of the paper against the safety pin and wrap it around the matchbox until it arrives at the other side of the pin.

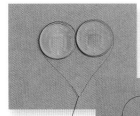

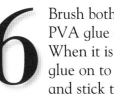

Mark a point that lines up with the middle of the coins. This will make the 'v' shape easier to draw.

If there are any gaps in the glitter, simply brush on a little more PVA glue and dip again!

Stick the heart on to the side that doesn't have the safety pin.

5 To draw the heart, take a stiff piece of card and place two small coins next to each other on it. Draw around the coins, and then a 'v' shape underneath them. Cut the heart shape out.

6 Brush both sides of the heart with PVA glue and dip it into some glitter. When it is dry, put a blob of PVA glue on to the front of the matchbox and stick the heart on firmly.

Close to the heart!

Now it's time to fill your matchbox! You could put a photo of yourself inside it for the person to wear near to their heart! Or you could write a secret letter or poem to pop inside.

Football crazy

Try painting a football box for a special footie-fan friend. You could fill it with pictures of their favourite team players.

Up, up, and away!

Why not make one for yourself? Design a special box and put a picture of your secret pin-up inside!

STONE WARNING

Do you ever want privacy in your bedroom to discuss secret plans? Here's a way to ensure that everyone enters with caution!

From card to carving

Squeeze the two sides together to cut the 'v' shape.

Do not force the crunching too much or the box will tear.

Materials

Cereal box, white paper, and newspaper

Sticky tape

Paint

Toilet paper

Glue mixture

Scissors

Pencil

Paintbrush

Marker pen

1 Take an empty cereal box and snip some 'v' shape slits along the edges with a pair of scissors. Don't snip too many slots down each edge.

2 Stand the box up and crush it down to buckle the sides. Stuff the box with crunched-up balls of newspaper. Tape the top down securely.

3 Decide at this stage what you want to carve into your stone slab. It's a good idea to practise first on a piece of paper. You could choose a message such as 'Beware Do Not Enter', or a picture such as a skull and crossbones.

4 Cover the box with PVA glue mixture and lay strips of toilet paper on the front. Lay six or seven layers down on the front only and make sure they remain wet and pulpy while you are covering it.

Caution!

Put your ancient stone warning slab outside your bedroom door to bar the way of anyone entering. A scary picture is guaranteed to work as a very effective warning!

Highlighting the indentations with black pen really makes the picture stand out.

For the best effect, use a darker version of the main colour in the carved areas.

Try adding some symbols or heiroglyphics to your design.

Tomb raider
You would expect to find this sand coloured slab in an Egyptian tomb, complete with a mysterious message!

Bat mania
Try a scary sign like these vampire bats. It will ensure that unwelcome visitors will knock first!

5 While the pulp is still wet, carve the picture into it, using a pencil. When you have finished, cover the rest of the box with PVA glue mixture and one layer of toilet paper. Leave it to dry.

6 When it is dry and rock hard you can make out the indentations of the carvings. Paint the surface using black and white acrylic or poster paints. Use darker paint in the carved grooves to highlight them.

WAX ILLUSION

Have you ever wanted to send someone secret instructions on how to find a hidden object? Here is a fantastic way to send an invisible map!

Materials

A4 paper and newspaper

Wax crayons and coloured pencils   Paint

Old ballpoint pen

Paintbrush

From invisible to visible

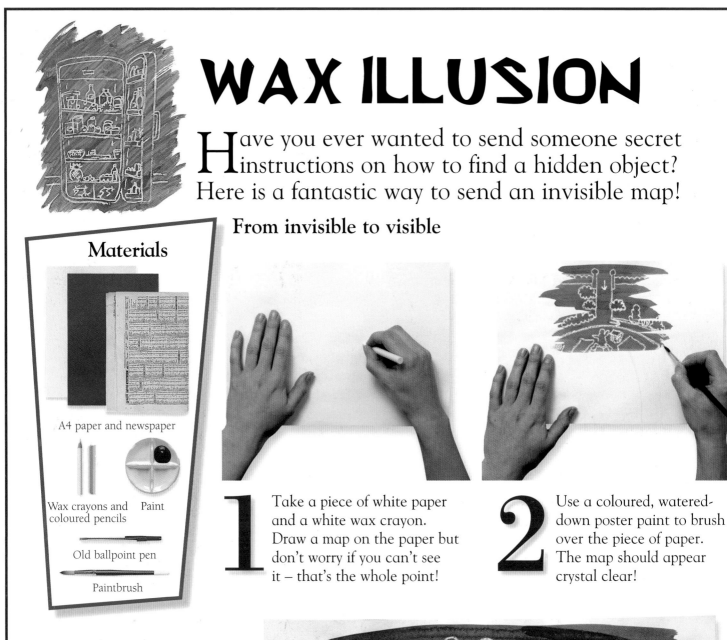

1 Take a piece of white paper and a white wax crayon. Draw a map on the paper but don't worry if you can't see it – that's the whole point!

2 Use a coloured, watered-down poster paint to brush over the piece of paper. The map should appear crystal clear!

The thinner the paint, the more effective it will be.

Mystery map

Mark the hiding place with an x on your map. Then send it to a friend – make sure they know how to read it first! Anyone else who gets their hands on the map will think it's just a plain piece of paper.

INVISIBLE MAP

What happens if someone finds out how to decipher the wax illusion? Don't worry – try this alternative invisible map instead!

From indent to illusion

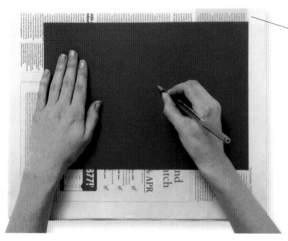

The newspaper will ensure that you can press hard enough to make the imprint without damaging the table beneath!

1 Lay a piece of A4 paper on an old newspaper. Take a ballpoint pen that has run out of ink and press a map hard into the paper without tearing it.

2 Take a coloured pencil that is a different colour to the paper. Rub the pencil all the way across the paper and the map should appear clearly! Try to do the rubbing evenly.

Hiding place
You could use the invisible map to show a friend where an object, such as a key, is hidden in your room. But remember to destroy the newspaper that you lean on – you might have transferred the secret map onto it and sombody could read it!

Make sure the pencil and paper are contrasting colours.

CLUB CARD

Now you have your secret club badges you need some form of official identification. Easy – simply make your own membership cards!

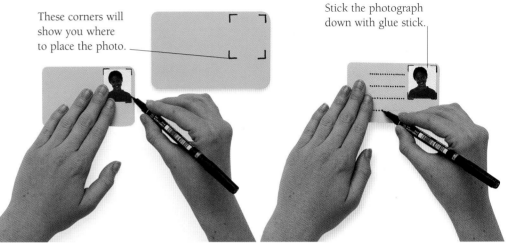

From card to club member

These corners will show you where to place the photo.

Stick the photograph down with glue stick.

Materials

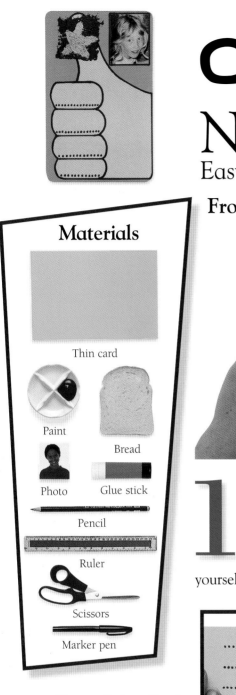

Thin card

Paint

Bread

Photo

Glue stick

Pencil

Ruler

Scissors

Marker pen

1 Cut a small rectangle out of thick paper or thin card, about the size of a credit card, and round off the corners. Take a small photograph of yourself and draw around the corners.

2 With a pencil, lightly draw four lines of equal distances across the card. Go over them with a marker pen, using dots rather than a thick line. Rub out the lines when the pen is dry.

Dip a small piece of bread in paint to stamp the bottom right hand corner.

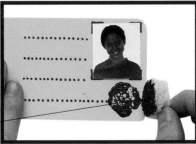

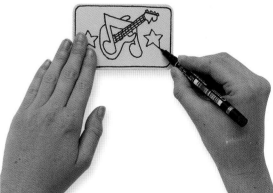

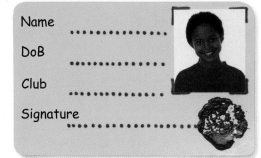

Name ....

DoB ....

Club ....

Signature ....

3 Write 'name', 'date of birth', 'club', and 'signature' down the left hand side of the card. Make a stamp in the bottom corner using a small piece of bread.

4 Decorate the back by drawing a design based on the theme of the secret club. When you have finished you can hand the cards out to the club members for them to fill in.

Club class

Now you have your own personal membership card complete with the details of your club. You shouldn't give away too many details, however, you want to keep it as secret as possible! Don't let a card fall into the wrong hands!

The back should give a small clue as to what the club is all about.

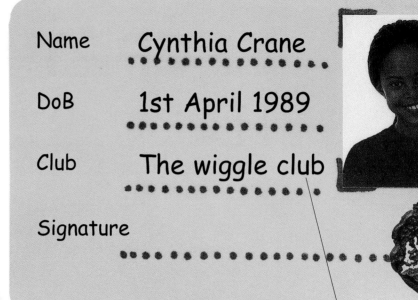

Name	Cynthia Crane
DoB	1st April 1989
Club	The wiggle club
Signature	

Call your secret club a name that doesn't tell people exactly what it is!

Covering up

You could always cover your official club card with sticky-backed plastic. This will help to preserve it and make it waterproof.

You can either use a passport photo or you can cut your head out of a larger picture.

Try using two colours for your stamp.

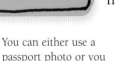

Use poster paints to add different colours to your cards.

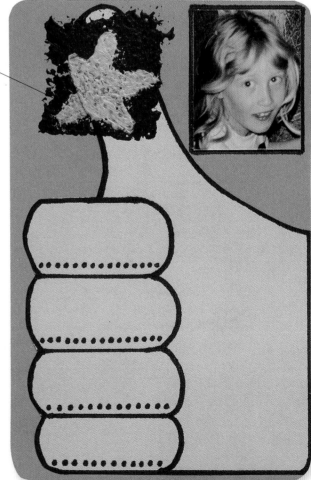

Key features

Membership cards come in all shapes and sizes. Why not try this key shape, the odder the shape the more it will mystify anyone who dares try and question the club without being invited to!

Thumbs up!

This handy image is perfect for an official card. Why not make up a password or even a special sign, such as this 'thumbs up' to alert other members to the fact that you belong to the same club.

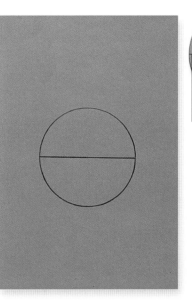

SECRET CODES

Ｈow would you like to make a completely deci-pher-proof code that only you and your best friend will be able to read? Now you can!

From card to code

Make the marks at 12 degrees, 24, 36, 48, 60 and so on until you reach the end.

Make sure the line goes straight through the centre.

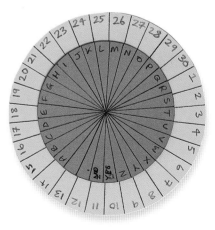

1 Take a piece of thin card and draw a circle on it with your compass. Mark the centre, and draw a line through the middle. Cut the circle out.

2 Place a protractor on the centre line and mark at 12 degree points around the circle. Turn it upside down and mark the rest of the circle.

3 When you have marked the circle all the way around, take a ruler and draw a line from the centre of the circle to each of the marks. When you have finished make another larger disc in exactly the same way.

The larger circle should be about 2 cm larger around the edge than the small one.

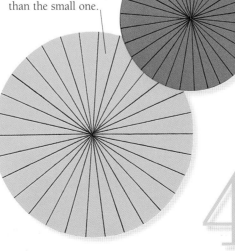

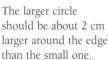

4 On the big wheel write the numbers 1-30 in each gap. In the small wheel write the letters A-Z and in the four gaps write 'no', 'yes', a 'fullstop' and leave one blank.

Code wheel

Now that you have your decorated secret code wheel all you need to do is work out how to use it! Turn the page to find out how to send messages that not even the cleverest of code-breakers will be able to decipher!

You could use coloured pens or pencils as well as paint to decorate.

Love wheel

If you use the secret code to send a secret message to a loved one, why not design a heart wheel like this one? You could use a silver pen for the numbers to make it really special!

It is very important that the 12 degree gaps are measured accurately so that the wheels match up.

Use a sharp pencil to make a clear hole.

Use poster or acrylic paints for the decoration.

Split the pin at the back of the circles.

5 Punch a hole through the middle of both of the circles with a pencil. Place a ball of sticky tack behind the cards when you poke the pencil through. Join them together with a split pin.

6 Now you have your secret code maker, you need to decorate it! Create your own design and paint it. Go over the numbers and letters with a marker pen.

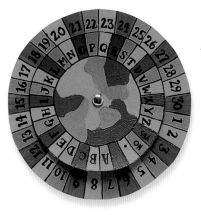

SECRET CODES

To make this brilliant code wheel work, your best friend will have to make one as well. You will need two exactly the same.

Code setting

When you have a code wheel each, you will be able to set the code with your friend. To translate your message, your friend will have to use the same code as when you wrote the note. On this wheel the code is set on **1** and **P**, so **1** equals the letter **P**. Now it is ready to use! Write a message using the numbers around the edge that apply to their corresponding letter. When you want to write a new word go to where the space is, here it is 15. You will now have a message written with just numbers!

Crack the cipher!

Your friend will be able to translate the message simply by using the same code setting on their wheel, which you have arranged beforehand. This message was set with the code wheel on the right. Practise a message using this wheel!

The letter 'J' will be written as '25'.

5,23,20,15,1,16,4,4,8,30,3,19,15,24,4,15,26,20,10

THE PASSWORD IS THE KEY

The '10' is a 'Y' on the code wheel.

! In on the secret
It is very important to tell your friend the code setting. Why not write the setting in the corner of the message?

5,23,20,15,1,24,22,20,30,29,15

23,16,4,15,27,20,21,5,15,5,23,20

15,18,30,30,1,14,15

28,20,4,4,16,33,20,15,5,30,15,18,30,28,20

Brain teaser

To practise deciphering, try working out this long message using the settings on the heart wheel to the left. The answer is under 'Message 1' at the bottom of the page.

Hieroglyphic wheel

You can also make a wheel with pictures and letters, instead of numbers. Try making this ancient Egyptian hieroglyphic wheel! Write a picture message to someone and if anyone else finds it there is absolutely no hope of them cracking the code unless they have the wheel and the setting!

You can choose any picture you want!

I LOVE YOU

Picture codes

Here is an example of a simple picture message, use the Egyptian wheel to crack it and check your answer below!

FORBIDDEN FILE

Do you have any private notes that you don't want anyone to see? If so, you need a secret file, or a secret compartment in a secret file!

From card to compartment

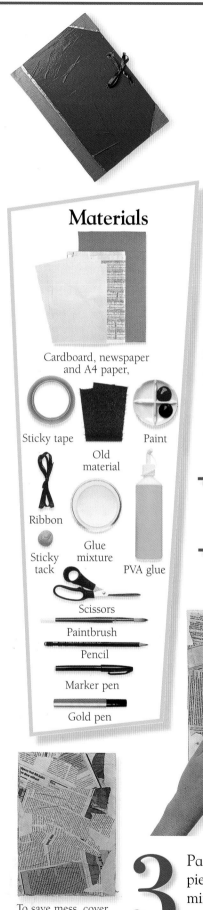

Materials

Cardboard, newspaper and A4 paper,

Sticky tape

Old material

Paint

Ribbon

Glue mixture

Sticky tack

PVA glue

Scissors

Paintbrush

Pencil

Marker pen

Gold pen

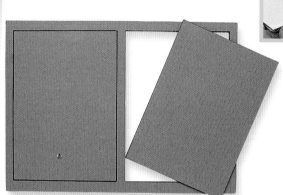

Use a long strip of sticky tape and curl it over the edge of the cardboard.

1 Take two pieces of A4 size paper and place them side by side on a piece of cardboard. Draw around the paper with a pen, and cut the shapes out.

2 Lay a piece of A4 paper on each piece of cardboard and tape them down. Only tape the top, bottom, and one side. Leave one side open.

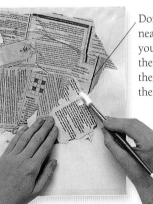

Don't be too neat when you lay on the strips – the wrinklier the better!

When the PVA glue dries it will be hard and shiny.

To save mess, cover one side at a time and let it dry!

3 Paint both sides of the cardboard pieces, or file flaps, with PVA glue mixture. Stick strips of newspaper all over both sides. Be very careful not to paste over the pocket openings.

4 When the file flaps are dry, paint them with brown paint for a leather effect. When they are dry, cover them with PVA glue, which will dry see-through.

Make sure there is a gap of about 1 cm between the flaps, so that the file will close.

Cut triangular pieces of material out for the corners and stick them on with PVA glue.

The ribbon should be long enough to tie a secure bow.

Make sure you use a sharp pencil to pierce the holes, but be very careful.

5 Place the two flaps side by side with the open pockets facing each other and the cardboard sides facing up. Lay a piece of material, about 4 cm wide, down the centre. Stick it down with PVA glue.

6 Pierce two holes with a pencil, using sticky tack to push in to, along the edges where the file opens. They should be roughly 5 cm apart and about 2 cm in from the edge. Thread a piece of ribbon through the holes.

For your eyes only

To finish the edges off neatly, use a gold pen to draw lines around the material and the holes. Paint 'Top Secret' on the front with acrylic paint to deter anyone curious enough to look at the contents. But even if they do take a peep, they won't spot the top secret compartments with your top secrets inside!

Splat attack!

Try your own designs, this Art Attack splat file is a perfect place to keep all your Art Attacks – You can hide the ones you will give away as presents!

You could use a stencil to give it a stamped look.

Gold and silver pen give a really good sparkly look!

Secret party details for Jackie's birthday
Balloons
Birthday cake
Games
Presents
Music
Magician
Party hats

List of people to invite:
Penny
Benjamin
Emma
Alison
Annette
Dean
Jim

Peeping Tom

Private documents will be safe and sound! No prying eyes will ever think to look for secret sleeves inside a file!

JUMBLE JIGSAW

When it's Valentine's Day, are you a little bit shy when it comes to what to write in a card? Here's an answer – a jumble jigsaw!

From jumble to jigsaw

Materials

Card and white paper

Coloured pens

Glue stick

Ruler

Pencil

Scissors

1 Take a sheet of A4 paper and lots of coloured pens, pencils and crayons. Write your message around the edges of the paper, turning it as you go.

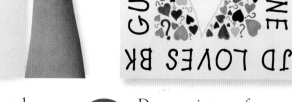

2 Draw a picture of a heart, or lots of hearts, in the middle of the paper. Add a question mark if you like!

It's up to you how many clues to your identity you give in your message!

Stick the picture in the centre of the card.

3 Using a ruler, draw a rectangle around the picture and cut it out. The picture and the message will now be on separate pieces of paper.

4 Fold a piece of thin card in half, making sure it is bigger than the rectangle you have cut out. Glue the heart picture onto it.

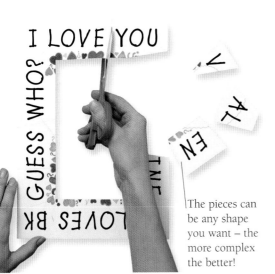

The pieces can be any shape you want – the more complex the better!

Make sure you put all the pieces into the card. You don't want any gaps in the jigsaw!

5
Take the piece of paper with the message on it and cut it into lots of pieces. You don't have to be particularly neat. This will make up the special jigsaw message!

6
Slip the pieces of paper into the centre of the card loosely, and send it to your valentine. When they receive it they will be able to piece it together to read the whole message.

Piece offering
What a surprise your valentine will get when the card opens and all the pieces fall out! And let's face it, if they go to those lengths to read your card, they must really fancy you!

Use as many different coloured pens and pencils as you can to make it really bright.

Try writing the message all over the paper including the cut-out part in the middle. You can cut the middle into any shape you want.

Cryptic message
You could use this jigsaw idea for other purposes too. Why not send your club members a jumble jigsaw with a secret meeting place hidden in the message?

INDEX

ACKNOWLEDGMENTS

Dorling Kindersley would like to thank the following people for their help in the production of this book: Suzanne Garton for making Art Attack material available; Penny York, Caroline Greene, and Lee Simmons for editorial assistance; Robin Hunter for computer graphics; Chloe Smith for modelling her hands and feet; Amy Junor for modelling her hands.